GW00499813

Super Easy Keto Crock Pot Cookbook

Lose Up To 5 Pounds In 5 Days With Tasty And Affordable Recipes. Discover How Simple Can Be Lose Weight Fast While Eating Awesome Food

Clara Smith

© Copyright 2021 - All rights reserved.

Table of Contents

Introduction

The crockpot has long been a favorite kitchen implement for the 'set-it-and-forget-it' meal. It's a wonderful invention by whoever thought it up, and it has saved many a few dollars on electricity by not needing to keep the stove and oven on for extended hours and all day. So, what really is a crockpot?

A crockpot is also called a slow cooker or a casserole crockpot. These nicknames refer to the same kitchen appliance, and it is one of the most used reheating methods today. It is basically a cooker with a glazed ceramic bowl that has a tight sealing lid. It is because of the liquid that will go in with the food. The crockpot is then plugged into an electrical socket in the kitchen for it to work.

The crockpot slow cooking method involves basically depositing the ingredients you desire to cook into the crockpot bowl (usually by stirring it with a wooden spoon or a ladle), adding the liquid of choice, cooking it for a few hours until it's done. These used to be the standard cooking methods in kitchens, and they have stayed the same with the invention of the crockpot. Nowadays, most crockpots have interiors thermostatically controlled to ensure that it's set at the right temperature during the cooking process to not over-cook your meals.

The best in crockpot slow cooking is finding that low and slow recipe. Recipes that are low in time length are usually very low in steps, and not much work is involved. It usually leads to the much sought after 'set it and forget it' kind of meal. Imagine not having to watch your meals cook slowly as you work on other tasks; you can avoid the temptation of peeking or checking on it too often and not having to worry about burning or crusting on the sides of your crockpot. When cooking at low heat, you don't have to worry about your meal exploding all over the kitchen or all the grease falling out and sticking to the bottom of your crock.

The best use of crockpot slow cooking is the convenience of the food, especially during holidays and parties. You can set the crockpot down on the table, and everyone can serve themselves. It is an excellent and great way to spend time with your guests and treat them well. There is nothing cheesier than eating the same dish fondue style. You get to enjoy slow cooking hotdogs for hours and hours without little ones surreptitiously taking off the top and poaching them in the pool of oil sitting beside the dish.

A crockpot is a very good way to use leftovers for a delicious meal. If you cook a large meal regularly and you have leftovers, put them in a crockpot with a liquid and let it cook. It will double the amount of food leftover or fed to the cat at the end of the week.

Crockpot cooking generally saves time, but it is also a low-budget way to cook. Slow cooking food can save you money because they are usually very low and easy to make. In fact, it is even possible to cook a meal with the last few pennies in your wallet. If you're on a tight budget and you don't have much to spend on your meals, the crockpot is the way to go.

Crockpots even make for a great gift since it's made in many shapes and sizes, from the really small, 1-quart crockpot to the huge 8 quarts or more. Any shape or size would be a welcome gift for anyone because everyone eats. Any occasion could be a good time to give someone a crockpot, and the more occasions you can name, the more crockpots you could make as gifts.

CHAPTER 1:

Breakfast

1. Zucchini Breakfast Casserole

Preparation time: 5 minutes

Cooking time: 4 hours

Servings: 8

Ingredients:

- 8 eggs, beaten

- 1 cup ricotta cheese, crumbled

- 1 cup parmesan cheese, grated

- Salt and pepper to taste

- 3 cups zucchini, grated and squeezed to remove excess water

- 1 ½ cup chopped plum tomatoes

- ½ cup fresh basil, chopped

Directions:

1. Mix all ingredients in a large mixing bowl until well combined. Place in a Ziploc bag and write the date when the recipe is made. Place inside the freezer.

2. Once you are ready to cook the meal, allow to thaw on the countertop for at least 2 hours. Pour the ingredients into the crockpot and close the lid. Cook on high for 3 hours or on low for 4 hours.

Nutrition:

Calories: 389

Carbohydrates: 6.3g

Protein: 27.5g

Fat: 36.3g

2.   Sausage and Kale Strata

Preparation time: 5 minutes Cooking time: 4 hours

Servings: 12 Ingredients:

- 12 eggs, beaten

- 2 ½ cups milk

- Salt and pepper to taste

- 2 tablespoons fresh oregano, minced

- 2 pounds breakfast sausages, sliced

- 1 bunch kale, torn into pieces

- 16 ounces white mushrooms, sliced

- 2 ½ cups Monterey Jack cheese, grated

Directions:

1. Mix all ingredients in a large mixing bowl until well combined.

    Place in a Ziploc bag and write the date when the recipe is made.

    Place inside the freezer.

2. Once you are ready to cook the meal, allow to thaw on the countertop for at least 2 hours. Pour the ingredients into the crockpot and close the lid. Cook on high for 3 hours or on low for 4 hours.

Nutrition:

Calories: 431

Carbohydrates: 4.5g

Protein: 32.3g

Fat: 37.4g

3.   Egg Cake Recipe with Peppers, Kale and Cheddar

Preparation time: 10 minutes

Cooking time: 4 hours

Servings: 6

Ingredients:

- 1 dozen eggs, beaten

- ¼ cup milk

- ¼ cup almond flour

- 1 clove of garlic, minced

- Salt and pepper to taste

- 1 cup kale, chopped

- 1 red bell pepper, chopped

- ¾ cup mozzarella cheese, grated

- 1 green onions, chopped

Directions:

1. In a mixing bowl, combine all ingredients. Place in a Ziploc bag and write the date when the recipe is made. Place inside the freezer.

2. Once you are ready to cook the meal, allow to thaw on the countertop for at least 2 hours. Pour the ingredients into the crockpot and close the lid. Close the lid and cook on high for 4 hours or on high for 6 hours.

Nutrition:

Calories: 527

Carbohydrates: 3.1g

Protein: 42.3g

Fat: 45.6g

4.   Feta Cheese and Kale Breakfast Casserole

Preparation time: 5 minutes

Cooking time: 4 hours

Servings: 6

Ingredients:

- 10 ounces kale, chopped

- 2 teaspoons olive oil

- ¾ cup feta cheese, crumbled

- 12 eggs, beaten

- Salt and pepper to taste

Directions:

1. Mix all ingredients in a large mixing bowl until well combined. Place in a Ziploc bag and write the date when the recipe is made. Place inside the freezer.

2. Once you are ready to cook the meal, allow to thaw on the countertop for at least 2 hours. Pour the ingredients into the

crockpot and close the lid. Cook on high for 3 hours or on low for 4 hours.

Nutrition:

Calories: 397

Carbohydrates: 4g

Protein: 32.2g

Fat: 29.4g

5.   Cauliflower and Ham Casserole

Preparation time: 5 minutes

Cooking time: 4 hours

Servings: 6

Ingredients:

- 1 head cauliflower, grated

- 1 cup ham, cubed

- ½ cup mozzarella cheese, grated

- ½ cup cheddar cheese, grated

- 1 onion, chopped

- Salt and pepper to taste

- 10 eggs, beaten

Directions:

1. Mix all ingredients in a bowl. Place in a Ziploc bag and write the date when the recipe is made. Place inside the freezer.

2. Once you are ready to cook the meal, allow to thaw on the countertop for at least 2 hours. Pour into the crockpot. Close the lid and cook on high for 3 hours or on low for 4 hours.

Nutrition:

Calories: 418

Carbohydrates: 5.2g

Protein: 28.1g

Fat: 42.4g

CHAPTER 2:

Mains

6.   Lasagna with Beef

Preparation time: 30 minutes

Cooking time: 4 hours & 30 minutes

Servings: 10

Ingredients:

- 1 tap dried oregano

- 1 chopped onion

- Ground Beef

- Minced garlic

- 1 can tomato paste

- 1 tsp salt

- Tomato sauce

- 1/2 cup parmesan cheese

- 1 Pack lasagna noodles

- Shredded mozzarella cheese

Directions:

1. In a large skillet over a medium heat, fry some beef with onion and garlic until slightly brown. Add tomato paste and sauce. Cook for 14 minutes, add oregano and some salt.

2. In a separate bowl, combine the cheeses and mix well. Grease your crock pot and place all the ingredients, in even layers, into it.

3. When all the layers are done, top the meal with cheese mix. Cover on low temperature mode for 4 hours and 30 minutes.

Nutrition: Calories: 446 Fat: 20g Carbohydrates: 35g Protein: 31g

7. Mexican Meat

Preparation time: 30-40 minutes

Cooking time: 8 hours

Servings: 12

Ingredients:

- 1 chuck roast

- 1 tsp ground pepper

- chili powder

- 1 onion

- Salt to taste

- olive oil

- Hot pepper sauce

- cayenne pepper

- garlic powder

Directions:

1. Remove all the excess fat from the roast and season meat with pepper and salt. Using a large skillet with olive oil, brown the roast from all the sides.

2. Cover the bottom of cooking dish some butter and place the roast into it. Add chopped onion, pepper sauce, powders and peppers. Pour in the water (slightly cover the roast) and cover the lid.

3. Set your crock pot on high for 6 hours. Then reduce to low and carry on cooking for another 2-4 hours (when meat easily fall apart). To serve, shred the roast with two forks and serve in tacos or burritos.

Nutrition:

Calories: 260

Fat: 19g

Carbohydrates: 3g

Protein: 18g

8.   Summer Pot Roast

Preparation time: 17 minutes

Cooking time: 7 hours and 30 minutes

Servings: 8

Ingredients:

- 4-5tbsp flour

- Pack beef mix

- 1 sliced onion

- 1 pack ranch dressing mix

- 1/2 cup water

- 1 pack Italian dressing mix

- Salt pepper

- 1 beef chuck roast (remove the bones)

- 5 whole and peeled carrots

Directions:

1. Cover the bottom of your cooking dish with butter or a little cooking spray. Place the sliced onion in an even layer onto the crock pot bottom.

2. Sprinkle the beef meat with species and rub into its surface. Roll meat in the flour just to cover from all sides. Place the meat into crock pot.

3. In a large bowl, combine Italian dressing mix, ranch dressing mix and beef gravy mix. Whisk and pour over the meat.

4. Place the carrots around the chuck roast. Set your crock pot on low mode and cook for around 8 hours until tender.

Nutrition:

Calories: 385

Fat: 22g

Carbohydrates: 20g

Protein: 23g

9.   Pork Chops in Sour Cream

Preparation time: 15 minutes

Cooking time: 8 hours

Servings: 10

Ingredients:

- 6 pork chops

- Garlic powder (to taste)

- 1/2 cup flour

- Salt

- 2 cups water

- Black pepper

- Container sour cream

- chicken bouillon

- Large onion

Directions:

1. Cover the chops with a spice mixture of pepper, garlic powder and some salt. Lightly brown chops in a large frying pan.

2. Cover the bottom of your cooking dish with some cooking spray and place the chops over it. Cover with onion.

3. Dissolve the cubes of bouillon in boiling water, and then pour the chops with this mixture. Cook, covered, for 7-8 hours on low. To serve, mix the sauce out of sour cream and 2 tablespoons flour.

Nutrition:

Calories: 257

Fat: 14g

Carbohydrates: 14g

Protein: 16g

CHAPTER 3:

Sides

10. Cabbage and Onion Mix

Preparation time: 15 minutes

Cooking time: 2 Hours

Servings: 2

Ingredients:

- 1 and ½ cups green cabbage, shredded

- 1 cup red cabbage, shredded

- 1 tablespoon olive oil

- 1 red onion, sliced

- 2 spring onions, chopped

- ½ cup tomato paste

- ¼ cup veggie stock

- 2 tomatoes, chopped

- 2 jalapenos, chopped

- 1 tablespoon chili powder

- 1 tablespoon chives, chopped

- A pinch of salt and black pepper

Directions:

1. Grease your Crock Pot with the oil and mix the cabbage with the onion, spring onions and the other fixings inside. Toss, put the lid on and cook on High for 2 hours. Divide between plates and serve as a side dish.

Nutrition:

Calories 211

Fat 3g

Carbs 6g Protein 8g

11.　Cauliflower and Potatoes Mix

Preparation time: 15 minutes Cooking time: 4 Hours Servings: 2

Ingredients:

- 1 cup cauliflower florets

- ½ pound sweet potatoes, peeled and cubed

- 1 cup veggie stock

- ½ cup tomato sauce

- 1 tablespoon chives, chopped

- Salt and black pepper to the taste

- 1 teaspoon sweet paprika

Directions:

1. In your Crock Pot, mix the cauliflower with the potatoes, stock and the other Ingredients, toss, put the lid on and cook on High for 4 hours. Divide between plates and serve as a side dish.

Nutrition: Calories 135 Fat 5g Carbs 7g Protein 3g

12. Broccoli Mix

Preparation time: 15 minutes Cooking time: 2 Hours

Servings: 10 Ingredients:

- 6 cups broccoli florets

- 1 and ½ cups cheddar cheese, shredded

- 10 ounces canned cream of celery soup

- ½ teaspoon Worcestershire sauce

- ¼ cup yellow onion, chopped

- Salt and black pepper to the taste

- 1 cup crackers, crushed

- 2 tablespoons soft butter

Directions:

1. In a bowl, mix broccoli with cream of celery soup, cheese, salt, pepper, onion and Worcestershire sauce, toss and transfer to your Crock Pot.

2. Add butter, toss again, sprinkle crackers, cover and cook on High for 2 hours. Serve as a side dish.

Nutrition:

Calories 159

Fat 11g

Carbs 11g

Protein 6g

13.   Roasted Beets

Preparation time: 15 minutes

Cooking time: 4 Hours

Servings: 5

Ingredients:

- 10 small beets

- 5 teaspoons olive oil

- A pinch of salt and black pepper

Directions:

1. Divide each beet on a tin foil piece, drizzle oil, season them with salt and pepper, rub well, wrap beets, place them in your Crock Pot, cover and cook on High for 4 hours.

2. Unwrap beets, cool them down a bit, peel, and slice and serve them as a side dish.

Nutrition: Calories 100 Fat 2g Carbs 4g Protein 5g

14.   Lemony Pumpkin Wedges

Preparation time: 15 minutes Cooking time: 6 Hours

Servings: 4

Ingredients:

- 15 oz. pumpkin, peeled and cut into wedges

- 1 tbsp. lemon juice

- 1 tsp. salt

- 1 tsp. honey

- ½ tsp. ground cardamom

- 1 tsp. lime juice

Directions:

1. Add pumpkin, lemon juice, honey, lime juice, cardamom, and salt to the Crock Pot. Put the crock pot's lid on and set the cooking time to 6 hours on Low settings. Serve fresh.

Nutrition: Calories: 35 Fat: 0.1g Carbs: 8.91g Protein: 1g

CHAPTER 4:

Seafood

15. Seafood Gumbo

Preparation time: 15 minutes

Cooking time: 5 hours

Servings: 6-8

Ingredients:

- 8-10 bacon strips, sliced

- 2 stalks celery, sliced

- 1 medium onion, sliced

- 1 green pepper, chopped

- 2 garlic cloves, minced

- 2 cups chicken broth

- 1 14-ounce can dice tomatoes, undrained

- 2 tablespoons Worcestershire sauce

- 2 teaspoons salt

- 1 teaspoon dried thyme leaves

- 1 pound large raw shrimp, peeled, deveined

- 1 pound fresh or frozen crabmeat

- 1 10-ounce box frozen okra, thawed and sliced into ½-inch pieces

Directions:

1. Brown the bacon in a skillet over medium heat. When crisp, drain and transfer to a crock pot.

2. Drain off drippings, leaving just enough to coat the skillet. Sauté celery, onion, green pepper, and garlic until vegetables are tender.

3. Transfer the sautéed vegetables to the crock pot. Add the broth, tomatoes, Worcestershire sauce, salt, and thyme. Cover and cook for 4 hours on low, or for 2 hours on high.

4. Add the shrimp, crabmeat, and okra. Cover and cook 1 hour longer on low or 30 minutes longer on high.

Nutrition:

Calories 273

Fat 8 g

Carbs 11 g

Protein 4 g

16.   Cajun Crab

Preparation time: 15 minutes

Cooking time: 3 hours

Servings: 5

Ingredients:

- 1 oz Butter
- 1 yellow onion
- 5 1/3 oz celery stalks
- 1 ¼ cups mayonnaise
- 4 eggs, freshly
- 2/3 lb. shredded cheese
- 1 lb. crab meat, drained
- 2 tsp paprika powder
- ¼ tsp cayenne pepper
- salt and pepper

For serving:

- 3 oz. leafy greens

- 2 tbsp olive oil

Directions:

1. Peel and chop the onion and celery finely. Take a medium-sized saucepan, add butter and roast a little onion and celery until translucent. Dress with salt and pepper at will.

2. Shred the cheese and set aside. Take another deep bowl, add mayo, freshly cracked eggs, crab meat, seasonings and 2/3 of the shredded cheese.

3. Add the fried onion and celery. Mix everything well and season at will. Open the Crock Pot and spray with the cooking spray finely. Pour the mix into the Crock Pot.

4. Add the remaining cheese on top and on low for 3 hours until golden brown. Serve with salad and black pepper! Bon Appetite!

Nutrition: Calories: 100 Carbs: 0g Fat: 1g Protein: 0g

17.   Smoked Mussels Crock Pot

Preparation time: 15 minutes

Cooking time: 3 hours

Servings: 9

Ingredients:

- 1 lb. Cauliflower

- ½ yellow onion

- 2 tbsp Dijon mustard

- 1 cup Mayonnaise

- 7 oz. shredded cheddar cheese

- 2 tbsp fresh chives (optional)

- 10 oz. mussels, canned

- salt and pepper

- Serving:

- 4 ¼ oz. Lettuce

- 4 tbsp olive oil

Directions:

1. Wash and cut the cauliflower into small florets and put them in a pot. Add water, it must cover the florets. Add salt and bring to a boil. Let the cauliflower boil for a couple of minutes.

2. Drain the cauliflower and discard the water. Peel the onion and chop the onion finely. Shred the cheddar cheese. Set aside.

3. Take a deep bowl, put the onion, mustard, mayo and 2/3 parts of the cheese in a bowl and mix everything well.

4. Open the Crock Pot, pour the mixture, add cauliflower and mussels. Cover and put on low for 3 hours. Once the dish is ready, sprinkle the remaining grated cheese on top and set on warm. Serve with lettuce.

Nutrition:Calories: 308 Carbs: 7g Fat: 25g Protein: 16g

18. Broiled Sea Bass with Chili Basil Glaze

Preparation time: 15 minutesCooking time: 4 hours Servings: 7

Ingredients:

- 2 tbsp Vinegar

- 1 tsp chopped basil

- 1/8 tsp red pepper

- 1 clove garlic

- ¾ tsp salt, divided

- 4 sea bass fillets (6-ounce)

- ¼ tsp black pepper

- Cooking spray

Directions:

1. Wash the fish fillet and dry it with a paper towel. Peel the garlic and mince. Wash fresh basil, chop finely. Crush the red pepper. Set aside.

2. Open the Crock Pot, spray with cooking spray the bottom and sides of it. Take a medium bowl, conjoin vinegar, basil, red pepper, garlic, salt.

3. Season the fillets with salt and black pepper at will. Place the sea bass fillets on a bottom of the Crock Pot, sprinkle with species.

4. Cover the lid and put on high for 4 hours or until the fillets are tender when tested with a fork. Bon Appetite!

Nutrition:

Calories: 208

Carbs: 11g

Fat: 3g

Protein: 0g

19.   Crock Pot Keto Sea Bass

Preparation time: 15 minutes

Cooking time: 3 hours

Servings: 5

Ingredients:

- 1 whole sea bass

- 1 tsp sea salt

- 3 sprigs fresh dill

- 2 sprigs fresh parsley

- lemon zest

- pepper at will

- Seasoning: 1 tsp sea salt + 2 tsp olive oil

Directions:

1. Shred the lemon zest in a plate. Set aside. Wash fresh parsley and dill. Wash the fish thoroughly, rinse well. Take off the scales, wipe dry.

2. Season with sea salt from both sides - inside and outside of the sea bass. Open the Crock Pot, spray with cooking spray the bottom and sides of it. Put the whole fish on the bottom of the Crock Pot.

3. Dress the fish with sprigs of dill and parsley. Put the lemon zest over the fish. Drizzle a little with olive oil.

4. Cover the lid and put on high for 3 hours, the sea bass must get tender when tested with a fork. Remove the fish carefully from the Crock Pot once the cooking time is over and serve on a plate.

Nutrition:

Calories: 580

Carbs: 88g

Fat: 15g

Protein: 22g

CHAPTER 5:

Poultry

20. Ranch Chicken

Preparation time: 5 minutes

Cooking Time: 5 hours

Servings: 2

Ingredients:

- 1 chicken breast

- 1/3 tbsp Ranch seasoning

- 2 cups broccoli florets

- 4 slices bacon, cooked and crumbled

- 1/4 cup mayonnaise

Directions:

1. Put the chicken in the crockpot and add the seasoning. Add some shallots to taste. Cover and cook for 4 hours on low.

2. Add the broccoli and cook for another hour on low. When cooked, add the bacon, mayonnaise, 1 tbsp vinegar and salt to taste. Stir well.

Nutrition:

Calories: 424

Fat: 23.3 g

Carbs: 4.8 g

Protein: 39.08 g

21. Salsa Chicken

Preparation time: 15 minutes

Cooking Time: 2 hours

Servings: 2

Ingredients:

- 1 chicken breast

- 1/2 cup fresh salsa

- 1/2 cup shredded cheese

Directions:

1. Lightly grease your crockpot with olive oil. Place the chicken breast in the crockpot and pour the salsa over it. Cover and cook for 2 hours on high.

2. When cook, top with cheese and bake for 15 minutes in a preheated oven to 425 F degrees.

Nutrition:Calories: 398 Fat: 18.3 g Carbs: 4.2 g Protein: 42.9 g

22.   Chicken Tikka Masala

Preparation time: 15 minutes Cooking Time: 6 hours

Servings: 2 Ingredients:

- 1 lb. chicken thighs, de-boned and chopped into bite-size

- 3 tsp Garam Masala

- 5 oz diced tomatoes

- 1/2 cup heavy cream

- 1/2 cup coconut milk

Directions:

1. Put chicken to crockpot and add grated ginger knob on top. Also add the seasonings: 1 tsp onion powder, 2 minced cloves of garlic, 1 tsp paprika and 2 tsp salt. Mix.

2. Add tomatoes and coconut oil. Mix. Cook for 6 hours on low. When cooked, add heavy cream to thicken the curry.

Nutrition:Calories: 493 Fat: 41.2 g Carbs: 5.8 g Protein: 46 g

23.   Lemongrass and Coconut Chicken Drumsticks

Preparation time: 15 minutes Cooking Time: 5 hours

Servings: 2 Ingredients:

- 5 chicken drumsticks, skinless

- 1 stalk lemongrass, rough bottom removed

- 1/2 cup coconut milk

- 1/2 tbsp coconut aminos

Directions:

1. Season drumsticks with salt and pepper. Place in the crockpot. In a blender, mix the lemongrass, coconut milk, coconut aminos, garlic and ginger to taste, 1 tbsp fish sauce and desired spices.

2. Pour the mixture over the drumsticks. Cover and cook on low for 5 hours.

Nutrition:Calories: 460 Fat: 39.7 g Carbs: 4.7 g Protein: 36 g

24. Bacon & Chicken

Preparation time: 5 minutes Cooking Time: 8 hours

Servings: 2

Ingredients:

- 1 chicken breasts

- 4 slices of bacon, sliced

- 2 tbsp dried thyme

- 1 tbsp dried oregano

- 1 tbsp dried rosemary

Directions:

1. Mix all ingredients in the crockpot. Add salt to taste. Cook for 8 hours on low.

Nutrition:Calories: 460 Fat: 39.7 g Carbs: 4.7 g Protein: 36 g

CHAPTER 6:

Meat

25. Shredded Beef

Preparation time: 5 minutes

Cooking time: 8 hours

Servings: 5

Ingredients:

- ¼ cup stock

- 4 pounds beef chuck roast

- salt and pepper to taste

- ½ teaspoon cumin

- ¼ teaspoon chili

- ½ tablespoon oregano

- ¼ teaspoon paprika

- 1/8 teaspoon cinnamon

- ½ teaspoon garlic powder

- 2 tablespoon tomato paste

- 2 cups water

Directions:

1. Place all ingredients in the crockpot. Cook for 8 hours on low heat. Once cooked, shred the beef with two forks. Serve with the juices of the beef roast.

Nutrition:

Calories: 339

Carbohydrates: 1.29g

Protein: 48.78g

Fat:15.46g

26.   Taco Meat

Preparation time: 15 minutes

Cooking time: 5 hours

Servings: 6

Ingredients:

- 1 tablespoon chili powder

- ½ teaspoon coriander, ground

- 1 teaspoon cumin

- ½ teaspoon dried oregano

- ½ teaspoon garlic powder

- ¼ teaspoon paprika

- ½ teaspoon onion powder

- ¼ teaspoon crushed red pepper

- 2 pounds ground beef

- 1 teaspoon salt

- 1 teaspoon black pepper

- 3 tablespoon tomato paste

Directions:

1. In a mixing bowl, mix together the chili powder, coriander, cumin, oregano, garlic powder, paprika, onion powder, and crushed red pepper. Set aside.

2. Season the ground beef with salt and pepper to taste. Rub the ground beef with the spice rub and place it in the crockpot.

3. Add the tomato paste. Cook on low for 5 hours. Once cooked, break up the meat with a slotted spoon.

Nutrition:

Calories: 399

Carbohydrates: 3.11g

Protein:38.9g

Fat: 24.8g

27.   Exotic Middle Eastern Beef

Preparation time: 20 minutes

Cooking time: 8 hours

Servings: 8

Ingredients:

- 3 pounds beef brisket

- Salt and pepper to taste

- 1 teaspoon fennel seeds

- 1 teaspoon whole cloves

- ½ teaspoon whole peppercorns

- 1 teaspoon cumin powder

- 1 teaspoon cardamom powder

- ½ teaspoon ground cinnamon

- 3 tablespoon tomato paste

- ½ onion, chopped

- 3 cups bone broth

- ¼ cup coconut vinegar

Directions:

1. Place all ingredients in the pot. Cook at low temperature for 8 hours. Once cooked, shred with fork.

Nutrition:

Calories: 563

Carbohydrates: 5.14g

Protein: 40.91g

Fat: 40.86g

28. Pot Roast

Preparation time: 15 minutes

Cooking time: 10 hours

Servings: 6

Ingredients:

- 2 pounds beef arm or chuck roast, trimmed from fat and patted dry

- 1 ½ teaspoon salt

- ¾ teaspoon black pepper

- 2 tablespoons basil, chopped

- ½ cup onion, chopped

- 4 cloves of garlic, minced

- 2 bay leaves

- 2 cup beef stock

Directions:

1. Place all ingredients in the crockpot. Close the lid and cook on low for 10 hours. Remove the bay leaves. Serve with the thickened sauce.

Nutrition:

Calories: 234

Carbohydrates: 2.4g

Protein: 33.1g

Fat: 10.3g

29. Tamil Attukal Paya Dish

Preparation time: 10 minutes

Cooking time: 10 hours

Servings: 10

Ingredients:

- 1 ½ pounds lamb fee, cut into chunks

- 1 onion, chopped

- 3 cloves of garlic

- 1 teaspoon black peppercorns

- 1-inch ginger, sliced thinly

- 1 can tomatoes

- 1 teaspoon coriander, ground

- ½ teaspoon cayenne pepper powder

- 1 bay leaf

- 4 cups water

Directions:

1. Broil the lamb fee first in the oven for 10 minutes to add a roasted flavor on the soup. Meanwhile, mix all other ingredients except the bay leaf and water in a food processor and pulse until fine.

2. Place the lamb feet in the crockpot and pour over the sauce. Add the bay leaf and water. Cook on low for 10 hours.

Nutrition:

Calories: 184

Carbohydrates: 2.27g

Protein: 17.06g

Fat: 11.51g

30.　Lamb Curry

Preparation time: 15 minutes

Cooking Time: 8 Hours

Servings: 6 – 8

Ingredients:

- 2 ½ lb. boneless lamb (shoulder is a good cut to choose for this dish), cubed

- 2 onions, roughly chopped

- 5 garlic cloves, finely chopped

- 4 tbsp curry paste

- 1 lamb stock cube

- 2 ½ full-fat coconut milk

- 2 tomatoes, chopped

- Fresh coriander, roughly chopped

- Full-fat Greek yogurt, to serve

Directions:

1. Heat some oil in skillet or pan. Add the lamb to the hot pan and seal on all sides, about 3 minutes. Drizzle some olive oil into the crockpot.

2. Add the lamb, onions, garlic, curry paste, salt, and pepper to the pot. Stir to coat the lamb in curry paste. Add the coconut milk, stock cube, chopped tomatoes, and 1 cup of water to the pot.

3. Place the lid onto the pot and set the temperature to LOW. Cook for 8 hours. Serve with a dollop of Greek yoghurt and fresh coriander.

Nutrition:

Calories: 144

Carbs: 7g

Fat: 6g

Protein: 14g

31. Beef Stuffed Mushrooms

Preparation time: 15 minutes Cooking Time: 3 Hours

Servings: 4 Ingredients:

- 1 cup cremini mushroom caps

- ½ cup ground beef

- 1 tablespoon butter, soft

- 1 teaspoon coriander, ground

- 1 teaspoon sweet paprika

- 1 teaspoon dried dill

- 1 oz Parmesan, grated

- ¾ cup of water

Directions:

1. In a bowl, mix ground beef, butter, coriander, dill and paprika. Fill every mushroom cap with the meat mixture and arrange them in the crockpot. Add water.

2. Top every mushroom cap with Parmesan and close the lid. Cook the mushroom caps for 3 hours on High.

Nutrition:

Calories 260

Fat 5.8g

Carbs 8.6g

Protein 7.4g

32.   Southwest Jalapeno Beef

Preparation time: 15 minutes

Cooking Time: 6 Hours

Servings: 4

Ingredients:

- 1 red onion, diced

- ½ green pepper, diced

- 2 oz. olive oil

- 10 oz. diced tomatoes

- 1 cup of carrots, diced

- 3 diced jalapeños

- 3 cup of cauliflower rice

- 3 cup of chicken stock

- 3 tablespoons of chili powder

- 1 tablespoon of salt

- 1 tablespoon of pepper

- 2 oz. diced cilantro

Directions:

1. Start by putting all the fixings into your Crockpot. Cover it and cook for 6 hours on Low settings. Once done, uncover the pot and mix well. Garnish as desired. Serve warm.

Nutrition:

Calories 391

Fat 21.8 g

Carbs 1.5 g

Protein 11.6 g

CHAPTER 7:

Vegetables

33.   Indian Eggplant Slices

Preparation time: 15 minutes

Cooking time: 2 hours & 30 minutes

Servings: 6

Ingredients:

- 2 medium eggplants, stem removed, cut into ½-inch thick slices

- 1/4 cup olive oil

- 1 teaspoon turmeric

- 1 tablespoon chili powder

- 1 tablespoon garam masala

- 1 tablespoon ground cumin

- 1 tablespoon chopped fresh cilantro

- 2 jalapeno peppers, seeded and minced

- 5 garlic cloves, chopped

- 1 teaspoon ginger paste

- 1 shallot, diced

- Salt, to taste

Directions:

1. Add all ingredients except the salt and cilantro into the crock pot and stir gently. Cover and cook on high for 2 hours, stirring after 1 hour.

2. If there is plenty of liquid after the 2 hour cooking time, cook on low for 30 minutes more to thicken. Add cilantro and salt and stir well. Serve and enjoy.

Nutrition: Calories: 106 Carbohydrates: 9.2g Protein: 1.7g Fat: 6.9g

34.   Delicious Veggie Mix

Preparation time: 15 minutes Cooking time: 6 hours

Servings: 4

Ingredients:

- 2 tablespoons olive oil

- 2 cups mushrooms, sliced

- 14 oz can tomato, diced

- 1 zucchini, chopped

- 1 green bell pepper, chopped

- 1/2 teaspoon dried oregano

- 1/4 teaspoon garlic powder

- Salt and pepper, to taste

Directions:

1. Coat the inside of the crock pot with the olive oil. Add all the

   ingredients to the crock pot and stir well. Cover and cook on low for 6 hours. Stir well and serve with keto-friendly breadsticks.

Nutrition:

Calories: 112

Carbohydrates: 8.3g

Protein: 2.9g

Fat: 7.5g

35.   Parmesan Garlic Mustard Greens

Preparation time: 15 minutes Cooking time: 3 hours

Servings: 4 Ingredients:

- 4 cups mustard greens

- 4 cloves garlic, minced

- ¼ cup Parmesan

- 1/3 cup almonds, sliced

- 3 tablespoons olive oil

- Salt and pepper, to taste

Directions:

1. Chop the mustard greens and toss with olive oil, salt, and black pepper. Place the almonds in food processor and chop.

2. Place the mustard greens in crock pot and top with almonds and parmesan. Cook on high for 3 hours. Serve warm.

Nutrition: Calories: 188 Carbohydrates: 5.4g Protein: 5.4g Fat: 16.1g

36.   Fragrant Radishes

Preparation time: 15 minutes Cooking time: 4 hours

Servings: 4

Ingredients:

- 20 radishes, stemmed

- ½ cup ghee

- 1 lemon, juiced

- ¼ teaspoon orange extract

- 1 tablespoon olive oil

Directions:

1. Place ghee in a small saucepan and melt over low heat. Remove ghee from the heat, add lemon, orange, and salt.

2. Add the radishes to ghee mixture and toss to coat. Place the radishes in crock pot and cook on low for 4 hours. Serve warm.

Nutrition: Calories: 270 Carbohydrates: 1.8g Protein: 0.3g Fat: 29.1g

CHAPTER 8:

Soups & Stews

37.   Chicken Soup

Preparation Time: 15 minutes

Cooking Time: 4 hours

Servings: 6

Ingredients:

- 1½ lb. cooked rotisserie chicken, shredded

- 2 (15-oz.) cans Great Northern beans, drained and rinsed

- 3 carrots, peeled and chopped

- 3 celery stalks, chopped

- 4 cups fresh baby spinach

- 1 yellow onion, chopped

- 3 garlic cloves, minced

- 2 bay leaves

- Salt and freshly ground black pepper, to taste

- 4 cups low-sodium chicken broth

- 2 cups water

Directions:

1. In a crock pot, place all the ingredients and stir to combine. Set the crock pot on "High" and cook, covered for about 3-4 hours. Serve hot.

Nutrition:

Calories: 377

Carbohydrates: 36.8g

Protein: 47.2g

Fat: 4.2g

38.   Best Dinner Option Soup

Preparation Time: 15 minutes

Cooking Time: 4 hours & 30 minutes

Servings: 4

Ingredients:

- 12-16 frozen turkey meatballs

- 1 (14-oz.) can chickpeas, drained and rinsed

- 2 medium carrots, peeled and chopped

- 1 medium onion, chopped

- 1 (28-oz.) can fire-roasted diced tomatoes

- 1 garlic clove, minced

- 1 tbsp. lemon zest, grated

- 4 cups chicken broth

- 1 (8-oz.) can tomato sauce

- ½ tsp. dried oregano

- ½ tsp. dried parsley

- Salt and freshly ground black pepper, to taste

- 2-3 cups fresh baby spinach leaves

- 1 cups orzo

Directions:

1. In a crock pot, place all the ingredients except for spinach and orzo and stir to combine. Set the crock pot on "High" and cook, covered for about 3-4 hours.

2. Uncover the crock pot and stir in the spinach and orzo. Set the crock pot on "High" and cook, covered for about 20-30 minutes. Serve hot.

Nutrition:

Calories: 845

Carbohydrates: 96.7g

Protein: 63.6g

Fat: 24.9g

39.   Meat Soup

Preparation Time: 20 minutes

Cooking Time: 4 hours & 30 minutes

Servings: 8

Ingredients:

- 1 lb. dried chickpeas, soaked for 12 hours and drained

- 2 lb. skinless chicken drumsticks

- 1 (4-oz.) piece Serrano ham, cut into ½-inch cubes

- 4 oz. Spanish chorizo, cut into ½-inch rounds

- 8 baby red potatoes, scrubbed and halved

- 2 medium carrots, peeled and cut into ½-inch chunks

- 1 large leek, (white and light green parts), halved and sliced thinly

- 2 celery stalks, chopped

- 3 large garlic cloves, minced

- 1 tbsp. fresh oregano, chopped

- 2 bay leaves

- 1 tbsp. smoked paprika

- ½ tsp. saffron threads

- Salt and freshly ground black pepper, to taste

- 6 cups hot chicken broth

- 1 lb. cabbage, cored and cut into 8 wedges

- ½ cups fresh parsley, chopped

Directions:

1. In a crock pot, place all the ingredients except for cabbage and parsley and stir to combine. Set the crock pot on "High" and cook, covered for about 4 hours.

2. Uncover the crock pot and with a slotted spoon, transfer the chicken breasts onto a cutting board. In the crock pot, place the cabbage and submerge into the soup.

3. Set the crock pot on "High" and cook, covered for about 30 minutes. Meanwhile, remove the bones from chicken breasts and cut the meat into bite-sized pieces.

4. Uncover the crock pot and discard the bay leaves. Stir in the chicken pieces and serve with the garnishing of parsley.

Nutrition:

Calories: 832

Carbohydrates: 78g

Protein: 65.2g

Fat: 29.2g

40.   Tuscan Dinner Soup

Preparation Time: 20 minutes

Cooking Time: 8 ¾ hours

Servings: 6

Ingredients:

- 16 oz. dried Great Northern beans, rinsed and drained

- 2 cups butternut squash, peeled and chopped

- 2 carrots, peeled and chopped

- 2 celery stalks, chopped

- 1 medium yellow onion, chopped

- 4 large garlic cloves, minced

- 4 fresh thyme sprigs

- 4 bay leaves

- Salt and freshly ground black pepper, to taste

- 8 cups chicken broth

- 1 lb. ground Italian sausage

- 4 cups fresh baby kale leaves

- 3 tbsp. tomato paste

- ¼ cups Parmesan cheese, shredded

Directions:

1. In a crock pot, place the beans, squash, carrots, celery, onion, garlic, thyme sprigs, bay leaves, salt, black pepper and broth and stir to combine.

2. Set the crock pot on "Low" and cook, covered for about 8 hours. Meanwhile, make small sized balls from the sausage and refrigerate before cooking.

3. Uncover the crock pot and transfer about ½ cups of the soup broth into a small bowl. In the bowl of soup, add the tomato paste and beat until smooth.

4. Add the mixture into the crock pot and stir to combine. Add the kale and sausage meatballs and gently, stir to combine.

5. Set the crock pot on "Low" and cook, covered for about 40-45

    minutes. Serve hot with the topping of Parmesan cheese.

Nutrition:

Calories: 447

Carbohydrates: 34.1g

Protein: 29.9g

Fat: 20.5g

41.   Pure Comfort Soup

Preparation Time: 20 minutes

Cooking Time: 8 hours 5 minutes

Servings: 10

Ingredients:

- 1 lb. ground Italian sausage

- 2 large carrots, peeled and chopped

- 2 celery stalks, chopped

- 1 onion, chopped

- 4 garlic cloves, minced

- 1 tbsp. Italian seasoning

- Salt, to taste

- 4 cups beef broth

- ¼ cups cornstarch

- ¼ cups water

- 36 oz. evaporated milk

- 12 oz. three cheese tortellini

- 5 cups fresh baby spinach

- 1 cups milk

Directions:

1. Heat a non-stick skillet over medium heat and cook the sausage for about 8-10 minutes. Drain the grease and transfer the sausage into a crock pot.

2. Add the carrots, celery, onion, garlic, Italian seasoning, salt and broth and stir to combine. Set the crock pot on "Low" and cook, covered for about 7 hours.

3. Meanwhile, in a small bowl, dissolve the cornstarch in water. Uncover the crock pot and skim off the fat from the top of soup.

4. Add the cornstarch mixture and evaporated milk mix until well combined. Add the tortellini and mix well. Set the crock pot on "High" and cook, covered for about 45 minutes.

5. Uncover the crock pot and stir in the spinach. Set the crock pot on "High" and cook, covered for about 10 minutes. Uncover the crock pot and stir in the milk, 1/3 cup at a time. Serve immediately.

Nutrition:

Calories: 439

Carbohydrates: 33.9g

Protein: 23.6g

Fat: 22.6g

CHAPTER 9:

Snacks

42.   Deviled Eggs

Preparation Time: 10 minutes

Cooking Time: 2.5 hours

Servings: 4

Ingredients:

- 2 eggs

- 1 cup water

- 1 teaspoon paprika

- ¼ teaspoon chili pepper

- 1 tablespoon butter

- ½ teaspoon minced garlic

Directions:

1. Place eggs, water in the crock pot, and close the lid. Cook the eggs for 2.5 hours on High. Peel the eggs and cut into halves.

2. Remove the egg yolks and place them in the blender. Add the paprika, butter, chili pepper, and minced garlic. Blend the egg yolks until smooth. Fill the egg whites with the egg yolk mixture. Serve!

Nutrition:

Calories 59

Fat 5.1g

Carbs 0.6g

Protein 2.9g

43.   Turkey Meatballs

Preparation Time: 15 minutes

Cooking Time: 3 hours

Servings: 6

Ingredients:

- 10 oz. ground turkey

- 1 teaspoon dried basil

- 1 teaspoon minced garlic

- 1 teaspoon ground black pepper

- ¾ cup almond milk, unsweetened

- 1 teaspoon oregano

- 1 tablespoon almond flour

Directions:

1. Mix the ground turkey, dried basil, minced garlic, ground black pepper, oregano, and almond flour. Stir the mixture until well blended.

2. Pour the almond milk into the crock pot. Make medium meatballs from the turkey mix and put them in the crock pot.

3. Cook the meatballs for 3 hours on High. Let the cooked meatballs cool slightly. Serve!

Nutrition:

Calories 190

Fat 14.7g

Carbs 3.2g

Protein 14.7g

44.   Chicken and Cauliflower Pizza

Preparation Time: 15 minutes

Cooking Time: 5 hours

Servings: 6

Ingredients:

- 3 oz cauliflower, chopped

- 4 tablespoons almond flour

- 1 egg, beaten

- ¼ teaspoon salt

- ¼ teaspoon ground black pepper

- 2 oz ground chicken

- 1 teaspoon butter

Directions:

1. Mix the almond flour and beaten egg. Add salt and ground black pepper. Knead into a smooth dough.

2. Roll out the dough in the shape of pizza crust. Rub the crock pot bowl with the butter and place the pizza crust inside the bowl.

3. Place the ground chicken on top of the pizza crust. Sprinkle the ground chicken with the chopped cauliflower and close the lid.

4. Cook the pizza for 5 hours on Low. Let the cooked pizza cool slightly then slice it into servings and enjoy!

Nutrition:

Calories 144

Fat 11.4g

Carbs 4.9g

Protein 4.8g

45.   Wrapped Prawns in Bacon

Preparation Time: 15 minutes

Cooking Time: 2 hours

Servings: 2

Ingredients:

- 6 oz. prawns, peeled

- 2 oz. bacon, sliced

- 1 teaspoon butter

- ¼ teaspoon minced garlic

Directions:

1. Mix the minced garlic and butter. Rub the prawns in the butter mixture. Wrap them in the sliced bacon.

2. Transfer the prawns to the crock pot and cook for 2 hours on High. Serve the cooked prawns and enjoy!

Nutrition: Calories 272 at 15.2g Carbs 1.8g Protein 29.9g

46.   Eggplant Fries

Preparation Time: 20 minutes

Cooking Time: 1 hour & 30 minutes

Servings: 4

Ingredients:

- 1 eggplant

- 1 teaspoon paprika

- ½ teaspoon turmeric

- ½ teaspoon salt

- 1 tablespoon butter, melted

- ¼ cup coconut flour

Directions:

1. Cut the eggplant into medium sticks. Sprinkle the eggplant sticks with the paprika, turmeric, and salt. Dip the eggplant sticks in the melted butter and coat in the coconut flour.

2. Place the eggplant sticks in the crock pot and cook for 1.5 hours on High. Let the cooked eggplant fries cool slightly. Enjoy!

Nutrition:

Calories 87

Fat 4.2g

Carbs 11.2g

Protein 2.3g

CHAPTER 10:

Desserts

47.   Lavender Blackberry Crumble

Preparation time: 15 minutes

Cooking time: 2 hours

Servings: 6

Ingredients:

- 1 1/2 pounds fresh blackberries

- 2 tablespoons cornstarch

- 1 teaspoon vanilla extract

- 1/4 cup white sugar

- 1 teaspoon dried lavender buds

- 1 cup all-purpose flour

- 1 pinch salt

- 1/2 cup butter, chilled and cubed

Directions:

1. Mix the blackberries, cornstarch, vanilla, sugar and lavender in your crock pot. Combine the flour, salt and butter in a bowl and rub them well with your fingertips until the mixture looks grainy.

2. Spread the mixture over the veggies and cook on high settings for 2 hours. Serve the crumble chilled.

Nutrition:

Calories: 140

Carbs: 26g

Fat: 5g

Protein: 4g

48.   Raspberry Brownie Cake

Preparation time: 15 minutes Cooking time: 3 hours Servings: 10

Ingredients:

- 1 cup butter, cubed

- 1 1/2 cups dark chocolate, chopped

- 1 cup sugar

- 4 eggs

- 1/2 cup cocoa powder

- 1/2 cup all-purpose flour

- 1 pinch salt

- 1 1/2 cups fresh raspberries

Directions:

1. Mix the butter with chocolate in a bowl and place over a hot water bath and melt them together until smooth. Remove the bowl from heat and stir in the sugar and eggs.

2. Add the cocoa powder, flour and salt and pour the batter in your greased crock pot. Top with raspberries and cover the pot. Cook on high settings for 3 hours. Allow the cake to cool before serving.

Nutrition:

Calories: 270

Carbs: 30g

Fat: 16g

Protein: 2g

49.   Banana Chunk Cake

Preparation time: 15 minutes

Cooking time: 3 hours

Servings: 10

Ingredients:

- 1/2 cup butter, softened

- 1/2 cup brown sugar

- 1/4 cup white sugar

- 2 eggs

- 2 tablespoons dark rum

- 1/4 cup milk

- 1 cup all-purpose flour

- 1 teaspoon baking powder

- 1/2 teaspoon salt

- 2 ripe bananas, sliced

- 1/2 cup dark chocolate chips

Directions:

1. Mix the butter and sugars in a bowl for a few minutes until creamy. Add the eggs, rum and milk and give it a quick mix.

2. Fold in the flour, salt and baking powder then add the banana and chocolate chips. Pour the batter in your greased crock pot and cook on high settings for 3 hours. Serve the cake chilled.

Nutrition:

Calories: 240

Carbs: 23g

Fat: 16g

Protein: 7g

50. Apple Butter

Preparation time: 15 minutes

Cooking time: 8 hours

Servings: 12

Ingredients:

- 4 pounds Granny Smith apples, peeled and cored

- 2 pounds tart apples, peeled and cored

- 2 cups white sugar

- 1 cup fresh apple juice

- 1 teaspoon cinnamon powder

- 1/2 teaspoon ground ginger

Directions:

1. Combine all the ingredients in a crock pot and mix well. Cover with a lid and cook on 8 hours. When done, puree the mixture with a hand blender and pour it into glass jars.

2. Seal the jars and store them for up to a few months in your storage room.

Nutrition:

Calories: 30

Carbs: 8g

Fat: 0g

Protein: 0g

Conclusion

You have to the end of this amazing cookbook, but always remember that this is not the end of your cooking journey with the crockpot; but instead, this is your stepping stone towards more cooking glory. We hope you have found your favorite recipes that are time-saving and money-saving.

Now that you know how Crockpot works and the many benefits of using it, maybe it is time for you to buy one for your family, in case you haven't owned one. When it comes to time spent preparing meals for your family, Crock-Pot is a lifesaver. If you are a busy person, a powerful solution is to use the crockpot.

You will also love to own one if you want to make your life simpler at work if you want to make your life simpler at home, and if you want to preserve some of the natural resources. You could also use one if you want to lean towards a healthier lifestyle as cooking in the crockpot is conducive to health than in the oven.

The crockpot can be used in making homemade and custom-made buffets, even in catering services. You can use it for cooking for your staff for special occasions and for showing them how to cook a tasty and healthier dish for your guests well within their own crockpot.

After choosing the best one for you, maybe it is time for you to know more about the recipes you should use. There are various recipes in this cookbook that are perfect for crockpot cooking, and they will definitely be useful and beneficial for you.

Moreover, whether you are a newbie or an experienced cook, you are going to love this cookbook as it is packed with every conceivable taste. You have discovered more than 1000 recipes in this cookbook that you can put into practice using your crockpot. You can always customize the recipes to suit your taste buds, as you can make any recipe mild or hot, sweet or sour; you have all the freedom to make the recipes your own. The best thing about cooking using a crockpot is that you just need to add the main ingredients, and no other complicated cooking preparation is needed; the crockpot will add most of the other ingredients for you.

CPSIA information can be obtained
at www.ICGtesting.com
Printed in the USA
BVHW091957220421
605650BV00002B/156